Strategy Management
A Pictorial Review of the ADEM Strategy Management Process

Dr. Mario D. Wallace

©Copyright 2020 by Mario Wallace

All rights reserved. No part of this publication may be reproduced, distributed, or transmitted in any form or by any means, including photocopying, recording, or electronic or mechanical methods, without the prior written permission of the publisher, except in the case of brief quotations embodied in critical reviews and certain other noncommercial uses permitted by copyright law. For permission requests, write to the publisher, addressed "Attention: Permissions Coordinator," at the address below.

All Things Strategic

PO Box 55661

Little Rock, Arkansas 72215

Allthingsstrategic.biz

Allthingsstrategic@gmail.com

Interior designer: Mario D. Wallace

Book cover: Mario D. Wallace

Wallace, Mario D.

STRATEGY MANAGEMENT

DEDICATION

This book is dedicated to my late mother and father, Deborah Ann Wallace, and Elias Muhammad. My mother always encouraged me to believe in myself and to pursue life with a passion while conquering my fears. My father instilled in me a passion for education and life learning. I miss them. I dedicate this book to my children for their patience with me throughout my 10-year educational journey. My children are the rock, and they keep me grounded and motivated to accomplish my life goals. Lastly, I dedicate this book to Orange Mound, the community where I was born and raised. Without the life experiences that I learned and earned in the Mound; I would not be the person I am today. Three fingers down and two fingers round.

STRATEGY MANAGEMENT

CONTENTS

Foreword	1
Purpose	3
ADEM Strategy Management Model	4
Research	6
Market Analysis	9
Executive Interviews	12
Focus Group Meeting	14
Town Hall Meeting	15
Strategic Vision	17
Change Agenda	18
Strategic Objectives	20
Strategy Map	21
Strategic Measures & Targets	22
Strategic Initiatives	24
Balanced Scorecard	26
Strategic Risk Management	29
Strategic Alignment	31
Cascading	33
Communication Plan	35
Change Management	36
Personal Scorecard	37
Governance Calendar	39
Strategic Review	40
Strategic Refresh	41
About the Author	43
Services	44

FOREWORD

If you decided to navigate a road trip through several states to see historic sites and eat amazing food, what would you use to ensure you did not get lost? The accessibility of GPS from cell devices to car computer systems makes such a journey highly feasible. Before GPS, people used physical maps to help ensure arrival at the desired destination. This is a simple illustration that highlights the fact that most of us understand, conceptually, to reach a destination there should be a plan. Using the same illustration, what would happen without any directions at all? Would you know what time you would reach the destination or if you would ever finally make it there? Even with road signs, you have no alert of closed roads a hundred miles ahead, or traffic delays, accidents, or multiple options for travel. While most of us would agree that it is wise to use a GPS when setting out into unknown territory, we often approach our goals in the workplace without direction, forethought, planning, or deadlines.

Strategic planning is an exercise that many executives have experienced. Groups get into a room and plan out the future so stakeholders can understand where the organization is going. Afterward, it is saved in a file and/or printed and bound neatly, only to be placed on the shelf. Occasionally, it may be referenced when someone wants to do something or before the end of the year to see if, by chance, something has been accomplished. While this is a common approach, it is definitely not the way to ensure that the desired goals are accomplished. So why do we keep doing it this way? Because it is easier to say what we are going to do than to actually track our progress with targets and measures; accountability makes people nervous, and it has always been done this way and to do it differently requires learning a new skill. Unfortunately, to be a truly effective executive leader, you must develop a skillful approach to strategy. Dr. Mario D. Wallace, the most advanced thought leader on strategic planning that I have ever engaged with, makes this process simple.

A true expert in any subject is easily identified in how simply they can convey complex concepts. Dr. Wallace has mastered the art of simplifying strategy, but he did not stop there. He also has created tools to empower the executive through strategy skill development. His thorough approach is broken down in the ADEM model and I know firsthand the power of the application. This is not a theory that was created in the lab and never put to real use in an organizational setting. Quite the contrary. This tool was created within the walls of a complex organization and use to help executives better understand how to work through the strategy process. Dr. Wallace's keen understanding of not only strategy, but also organizational development, training, and teaching has given him a unique ability to coach executives to greatness.

With his model, I was able to accomplish 87% of the goals I was responsible for leading, propelling me quickly through the ranks in my career and increasing my executive skill in strategy. Using his methods, I was able to empower my staff to lead specific aspects of the plan, which helped them take ownership and confidently communicate their progress every quarter. This approach not only helps you become a strategic leader. It also helps you develop others in ways that they can easily see how their contribution is aiding in the goal attainment. Dr. Wallace's brilliance in the design of such a powerful model, ADEM, is now at your fingertips. All you have to do now is turn the page, commit, and make it happen.

— Dr. Amber Smith, PhD

PURPOSE

Strategy Management: A Pictorial Review of the Strategy Management Process is the second book about the ADEM Strategy Management Model (ADEM model). The book provides an interesting and brief overview of the competitive strategy management process. The book uses pictures to visually communicate the steps in the strategy management process including brief descriptions that provide clarity of the process.

The book is used as a quick visual guide for leaders and strategy managers to reference as they apply the ADEM model in their firm. The goal of the book is twofold: 1) to assist leaders by increasing their depth of knowledge and application of the strategy management process and 2) to re-invigorate and encourage leaders across industries to return to strategic management.

This book is formatted into phases and elements of the ADEM model. The book was organized this way to enhance a leader's memory of the ADEM process. All the examples used in this book comes from the Arkhan case study that is referenced in my book *Strategy Is Spelled ADEM*.

Since you purchased this book, I assume that you already know strategy management, but you want to be able to engage in the process practically and effectively. If my assumptions are correct, this book is the perfect guide for you.

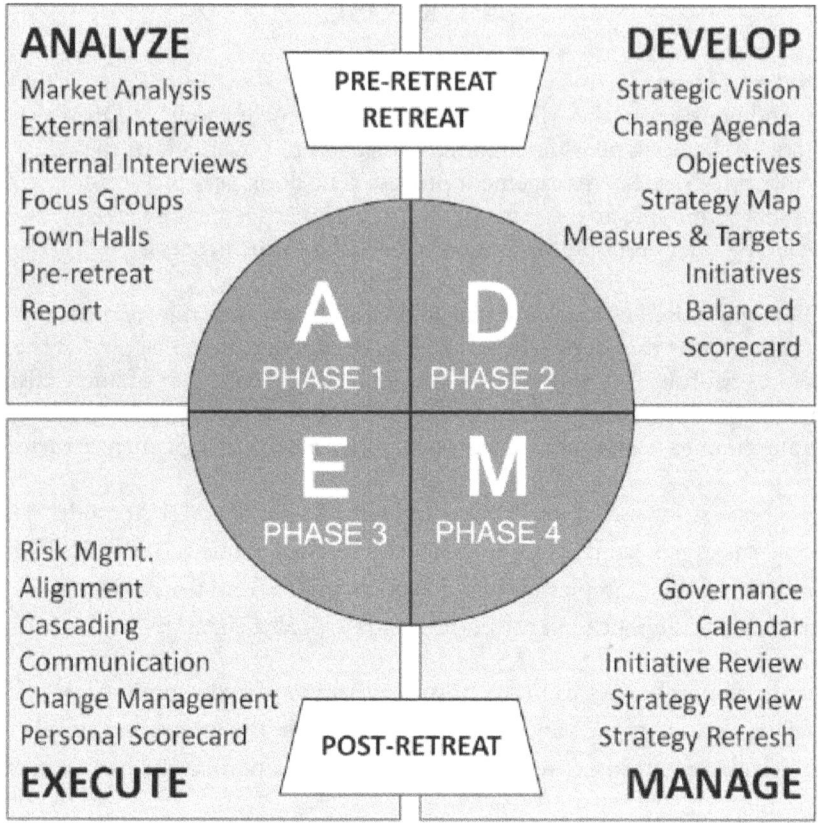

THE ADEM STRATEGY MANAGEMENT MODEL

The ADEM model is a strategy management framework for busy leaders that offer a linear approach to the strategy management process. The ADEM model is adaptive in the application and helps simplify the elements of the Balanced Scorecard (BSC) and any other strategy management process. The model was designed to engage busy leaders across industries and help them implement an organized approach to strategy management and reduce the chance of shelving the strategic plan. The acronym stands for the four identified phases of strategy management: Analyze, Develop, Execute, and Manage. Each phase has actionable elements that are dependent on the phase and interdependent on the elements across the model. Refer to Table below for the description of the phases.

A	Analyze	Making rational and strategic decisions by analyzing operational and marketing data, avoiding biases in the data, and choosing the most competitive strategic direction for the organization.
D	Develop	Translating operational and market data into a concrete plan that is adaptive to the market and considers the alignment of human capital, human capabilities, technology, and culture as factors of advancing the mission of an organization.
E	Execute	Effectively communicating the strategic direction while implanting strategy into the culture of the organization via aligning employees to the strategy, the strategy to employee performance, and effectively managing employee resistance.
M	Manage	Setting periodic strategic meetings to discuss strengths, weaknesses, opportunities, and threats and track a company's output and performance against regularly scheduled targets.

RESEARCH

The ADEM model evolved from an 18-month independent research study that involved a sample of 35 busy leaders from across institutions within higher education and the healthcare spectrum in Arkansas and Tennessee. The study included an equal balance of executive leaders and middle-level leaders. During the research period, leaders were consulted on strategic planning, some participated in a retreat, and some participated in leadership workshops. They all developed a strategic plan using the BSC methodology.

The findings of the research showed that busy leaders became mentally exhausted with the complex, multilayered process and felt a lack of control. Many of the executives completed the analysis and development phases of their plan then later either shelved the plan or handed it off to leaders who were not involved in the initial planning phases of the strategic plan.

The outcome of the analysis and development phases of each leader's strategic planning was highly effective. The execution rate of each leader's plans was extremely low. The management phase of each leader's plan was nonexistence. As a result, the four phases of the ADEM model evolved into a practical application for busy leaders to give them an organized, structured, and linear process to increase their chances of strategy execution. The ADEM model is designed to communicate to leaders that there are four phases in the strategy management process (i.e., Analyze, Develop, Execute, and Manage) and that all four phases must be processed accordingly.

ANALYZE

MARKET ANALYSIS

The analysis phase of the ADEM model consists of five elements: market analysis, external interviews, internal interviews, focus groups, and town halls. The most critical element of the five elements is market analysis. If a market analysis (environmental scan) is poorly executed, then the entire strategy will be worthless.

Analyzing the market involves being able to interpret large sums of data to seize market opportunities and determine a direction. To perform these tasks, leaders must analyze market share and outmigration trend data; competitor activities, and anticipated strategies, competitors, and major trends impacting their business. To highlight the approach that I used at Arkhan, please reference the Table below.

To complete a high overview for a market analysis at Arkhan, I created the CERD Analysis (i.e., Clinical, Education, Research, and Digital Health). For leaders at Arkhan. They needed an instrument that could help them scan the market environment from not only a macro scan, but also from a mission-specific focus that included a systematic process that leveraged their quadripartite mission areas. The CERD Analysis satisfied this need for leaders at Arkhan.

Clinical	Education	Research	Digital Health
<ul><li>Variation in health outcomes</li><li>Stroke rate and therapy</li><li>Highest obesity rates</li><li>Type II diabetes</li><li>Reduce readmission rates</li><li>Health professional shortage areas</li><li>Diverse workforce</li></ul>	<ul><li>Maximize innovation - active learning and Interprofessional Education</li><li>GME slots in Arkansas</li><li>Graduate readiness</li><li>Health professional shortage areas</li><li>Student recruitment and retention</li></ul>	<ul><li>NCI designation</li><li>Cancer researchers</li><li>Extramurally funded faculty</li><li>Peer-reviewed cancer-related funding</li><li>Collaborative cancer-related grants</li><li>Therapeutic clinical trials</li></ul>	<ul><li>Digital health infrastructure across Arkansas</li><li>Digital health competencies</li><li>New clinical services will be utilizing digital health</li><li>Alignment with care providers in rural Arkansas</li></ul>

Additional focus areas for a market analysis to consider:

- Population, demographics for targeted segmentation
- Market share and outmigration trend data
- Competitor activities and anticipated strategies
- Major trends impacting the industry

STRATEGY MANAGEMENT

- Physical plant (anticipated future needs)
- Potential alliances and geographic footprint expansion opportunities

EXECUTIVE INTERVIEWS

Executive interviews are designed to discuss the future direction (strategic horizon) of an organization provided that the executives' ideas carry tremendous weight. Executive interviewing expands the peripheral vision of the organization by engaging executives, board members, and other stakeholders in the interview process.

The goal of executive interviews is to provide critical insight for developing a strategic plan by soliciting insight and perspective on trends, threats, opportunities; explore data gaps, etc. Executive interviews also identify internal factors impacting a firm.

To effectively engage in this process, executive interviews must be scheduled and arranged with the most influential and impactful executives as identified by the Chief Executive Officer (CEO), Chancellor, or President (i.e., senior leadership, board members, physician leaders, others).

To accelerate the interview process, use audio transcribing technology such as Temi artificial intelligence (www.temi.com) to record the interviews. Artificial intelligence will increase the accuracy of the transcribed information and reduce the transcription processing time so that you can focus more on the data analysis.

FOCUS GROUP MEETING

The focus group related to the ADEM model is specifically designed to engage in the thoughts of middle management. The purpose of the focus group is to gather information from middle managers in a planned discussion regarding trends, threats, opportunities, and gaps in the existing operations. The goal is to gain buy-in from middle management and to begin mitigating potential resistance. The focus group is also designed to identify other factors impacting a firm including the strategic readiness of the managers to assist in carrying out the strategic plan.

To effectively engage in this process, conduct at least four focus groups with selected middle managers; solicit insight and perspective on future strategies regarding a firm's ability to respond to trends, threats, opportunities; explore data gaps, etc.; identify other factors impacting the firm. Analyze and code data responses from the focus groups.

To accelerate the focus group, use audio transcribing recording technology to ensure the accuracy of the information and to reduce the transcription processing time so that you can focus more on the data analysis.

TOWN HALL MEETING

The town hall meeting is specifically designed for engaging frontline staff and employees although middle management is welcomed. The goal of the town hall session is to collect information to inform frontline employees about the strategic plan, to get their buy-in, and to begin the process of mitigating potential resistance.

There should be multiple town hall meetings scheduled using a technology that can capture data. Poll Everywhere technology is a great tool to use in this setting. There should be less than 10 polling questions. Include at least two trivial questions as ice breakers to warm up the room.

Analyze and the code data responses from the polling data including data from the market analysis, the executive interviews, and the focus groups. Use all this data to draft the strategic vision of the firm.

DEVELOP

By 2029, ArKhan will lead the state to be the healthiest state in the region through its synergies of education, clinical care, research, and purposeful leadership.

STRATEGIC VISION

A strategic vision has a lifespan and a destination. It does not describe the purpose of an organization; it communicates the desired direction of an organization. A strategic vision is the Achilles heel in the process of strategy management. It can give a company a competitive advantage, differentiates the firm from its competitors, and can translate strategy into actionable steps. According to Davenport, Kaplan, & Norton, translating strategy into actionable steps for an organization begins with the strategic vision.

The strategic vision has three elements that include a strategic horizon, a niche, and a bold direction. The strategic vision example above includes the three elements: a strategic horizon (by 2029); a niche – regional focus using the synergies of education, clinical care, research, and purposeful leadership; and a bold direction – the healthiest state in the region.

You must work together with a diverse group of leaders to draft a strategic vision. Keep in mind that after a strategic vision is drafted, it must be translated into a change agenda to begin the process of communicating organizational changes and developing a strategic plan.

Domain(s)	Present 2018	To
Access to care	Shortage of medical professionals in rural regions in Arkansas. Uptick in healthcare disparities in Southeast Arkansas. Increase in emergency room visits. High percent of patients without PCPs.	Establish new access points in dense, rural population to improve health outcomes in underserved locations.
Medical professional model	Physician-centered model is ineffective and financially detrimental to the existence of the healthcare system.	Purpose-centered model with APRNs and PAs that meets the appropriate ratio of APRNs and PAs to MDs.
OBGYN	Nonexistent in the delta region.	Partner with the hospital best-suited to grow the program and impact OBGYN in the region.
Operations (i.e., productivity, quality, and lead "cycle" time)	Extremely long wait times in all clinics and low patient outcomes. Patient experience scores are low compared to competitors.	Increase in quality and patient experience scores including optimized patient throughput.

CHANGE AGENDA

A change agenda (CA) is a one-page document that communicates the current state of business domains (activities) and their desired future state. A CA articulates the actions that a firm must take to move from its current state to its desired future state. A CA must be socialized with employees across an organization for feedback before developing a strategic plan. After socializing the CA, leaders must approve it before using it to develop a strategic plan.

The lack of socializing the plan with employees across a firm can create an undesirable outcome and minimize efforts in the execution phase of the strategy management process. The development of the CAs is an imperative step in initiating the development of objectives.

You must work together with a diverse group of leaders in your firm to translate the strategic vision into a change agenda. You must articulate the actions that the firm must take to move from its current activities to desired future activities.

Characteristics of a Strategic Objective	Example
Written in the active voice (Directional-Verb-Noun Clause)	Increase (DV) Patient access to care in rural Arkansas (NC).
Directional short-term and long-term (Up, down, or around)	Increase, decrease, grow, enlarge, expand, etc.
Measurable	Expand rural clinics' footprint. **Measure:** Eight new rural clinic sites by 2025.

STRATEGIC OBJECTIVES

Strategic objectives are bold directional statements that must align with a strategic vision and indicate a strategic position in the market. The purpose of strategic objectives is to determine actions to achieve the strategic vision and mobilizing resources to execute the actions. Each strategic objective of a strategic plan must be scrutinized, and scrutinized, and scrutinized until they are perfect for the strategy.

The ADEM model focuses on two classifications of strategic objectives: corporate (parent) strategic objective and business unit strategic objectives. The parent strategic objectives focus on increasing shareholder returns, diversifying business activities, aligning a firm, and setting the competitive direction for a firm. The business unit objectives are more operational and focus on improving quality outcomes, driving efficiencies, engaging employees, and employee development. Business unit objectives in a firm must be aligned with the parent objectives to help mobilize resources and create synergy in a firm.

Once the strategic objectives are developed, they should be populated into the four perspectives of a strategy map in a way that creates alignment and synergy across the strategy. This step is better completed by someone who is disciplined in the BSC methodology, but anyone with executive fortitude should be able to do it. If there are any gaps in the strategy, the gaps become apparent at this point.

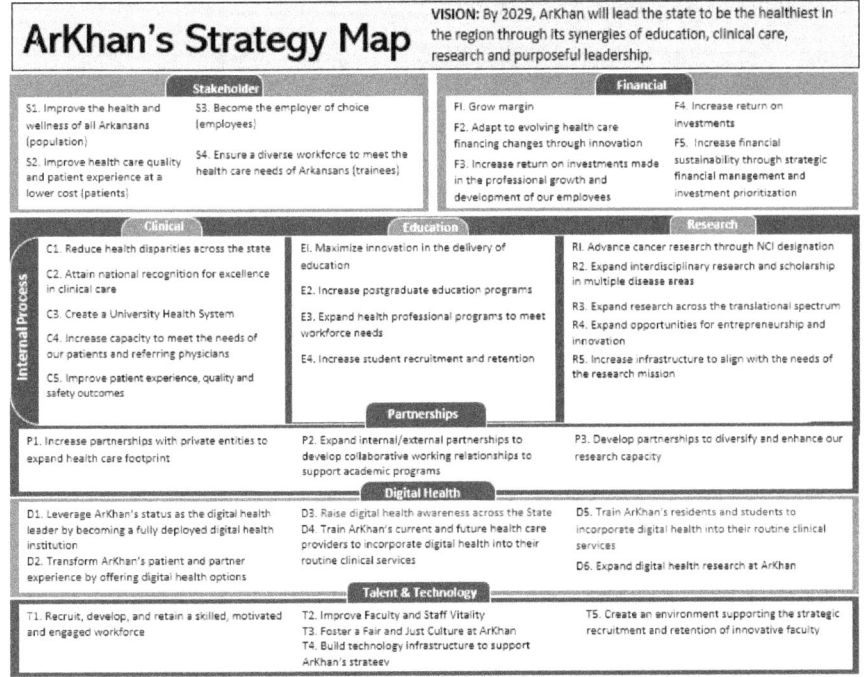

STRATEGY MAP

A strategy map is a one-page cause and effect diagram that communicates a strategic plan. It consists of four perspectives: financial, stakeholders, internal process, and talent & technology. The financial perspective includes objectives that support the short- and long-term return on investment and return by the institution. The stakeholder perspective includes objectives that contribute to the institution's value proposition for stakeholders (e.g., patients and family, students, and employees). The internal process perspective includes objectives that support the creation and delivery of value to stakeholders. The talent & technology perspective includes objectives that support the human capital, technological capital and cultural capital that drives performance improvement.

The strategic objectives must be placed in the appropriate perspective and have a perfect alignment on the map to create synergy. Synergy is the creation of a whole that is greater than the simple sum of its parts. The term synergy comes from the Attic Greek word and means "working together". The goal of the alignment is to create synergy across the map.

Objective: Maximize research funding threefold by 2024.			
Desired Behavior?	Increase number of faculty with intermural funding	Increase # of active clinical trials	increase collaborative research
What to measure?	Leading: Number of submissions and budget	Lead measure # open clinical trials, # of enrolled subjects	leading measure: # transdisciplinary submissions and associated budget
Type of Measure?	Lag Measure # of funded submissions and budget	Lag: clinical trial expenditures	Lag: # funded transdisciplinary submissions and budget
Category?	Percent increase	Percent increase	Submission number

STRATEGIC MEASURES & TARGETS

Measures are metrics that measure the progression of the strategy. There are two types of measures: lead and lag. Lead measures account for day-to-day progression. They are considered drivers because they drive operational performance toward strategic outcomes. Lag measures account for desired strategic outcomes. They are measured once a year or at the end of the strategy period. The six categories of measures are percent, ratios, indices, ratings, raking, and numbers. See the Table below.

Absolute number - (i.e., 1, 2, 3, 4)	Indices - Index of Data
Percent - 10%, 20%, 30%	Rating - 1 – 5; 1 – 10
Ratio - 5/10; 1/4; 2/1	Ranking - Low to High; 1st – 5th

Targets are the desired expectations to measure. There are three types of targets: look forward, look backward, and look around. See the Table below.

Look forward is a target that is created to defy the market; this type of target is not designed for comparison. It is designed to lead the market. Look backward is a target that considers historical data to determine the desired future expectation. Look around is a target that compares competitors' benchmarks to determine the desired future expectation.

Approach	Targeted Setting Method	Measure	Baseline	Year 1
Look forward	Derived from an overall business goal	Revenue	$3 Million	$4.5 Million Stretch goal
Look backward	Incremental improvement based on historical performance	Patient readmission rate	45%	30%
Look around	Benchmark industry of local competitor's medical school - IPE offerings are 25% in all programs	Interprofessional Education (IPE) offering	10% in all programs	25% in all programs

Characteristics of a Strategic Initiative	Example
Written in the passive voice (Noun Clause-verb)	Online onboarding portal development
Short-term and long-term where the verb or intransitive verb comes after the noun-clause	Enlargement, initiative, development, implementation, growth, etc.
Action oriented that includes a sponsor, a budget, a timeline, and a start and end date	Service line restructure initiative Digital health implementation project
Measured by percent complete, not by a measure and target	Service line restructure initiative 50% complete Digital health implementation project 25% complete

STRATEGIC INITIATIVES

Strategic initiatives are projects that have a beginning and ending date. They include team leads, resources, project managers, and change managers. A strategic initiative is the only action in a strategic plan, whose role is to move strategic measures toward their targets. Once a measure and a target are identified and fully developed, strategic initiatives are created, and mapped to an objective(s), prioritized, and funded.

According to Kaplan and Norton, in a strategy-focused organization, the balance sheet should include a budgetary line item for strategic initiatives that identifies the funding source. This concept is called StratEx. When initiatives are funded at the organizational level, this indicates to leaders in an organization that the budgeted initiatives have a fair chance of being implemented.

A strong strategic initiative is one that can support multiple strategic objectives in a strategic plan. A weak strategic initiative is one that only supports one strategic objective in a strategic plan.

Objective(s)	Measure(s)	Target(s)	Strategic Initiative(s)
Financial			
FI. Grow margin	Increase overall margin.	Increase 8%.	
Stakeholder			
S1. Improve the health and wellness of all Arkansans (population)	Ensure primary care access for all Arkansans.	Reduce the service gap by 65%.	Establish primary care access gap for all Arkansans.
Internal Process			
C1. Reduce health disparities across Arkansas	Mitigate Social Determinants of Health (SDOH) needs for patients.	Screened all patients for SDOH.	Establish an Office of SDOH.
Talent & Technology			
T1. Recruit, develop, and retain a skilled, motivated, and engaged workforce	Ensure all employees earn above a living wage.	100% of employees will earn above a living wage.	Perform ongoing, perpetual evaluation to assure all employees earn above a living wage.

BALANCED SCORECARD

Authored by Drs. Richard Kaplan and David Norton in 1992, the BSC is a complex, multi-dimensional strategy system that not only measures financial tangible outcomes, but also non-financial intangible drivers. It is designed to translate a strategic vision into organizational performance metrics for executing and operationalizing the strategic priorities of an organization. The BSC organizes the strategic priorities into a complex matrix called a strategy map. A strategy map is a one-page cause and effect diagram that communicates the strategic plan. It includes a strategic vision and four perspectives: financial, stakeholders, internal process, and talent & technology.

The financial perspective includes objectives that support the short- and long- term return on investment and return by the institution. The objectives in the financial perspective measure the added economic value to the institution. The stakeholder perspective includes objectives that contribute to the institution's value proposition for stakeholders (e.g., patients and family, students, and employees). The value proposition is a promise of value to be delivered, communicated, and acknowledged to the stakeholders. The objectives in the stakeholder perspective measure the outcome value of the promise.

The internal process perspective includes objectives that support the creation and delivery of value to stakeholders. The talent & technology perspective includes objectives that support the human capital, technological capital and cultural capital that drive performance improvement. The objectives in the talent and technology perspective measure the development and effectiveness of the human capital, technological capital, and the cultural performances of the institution.

In essence, the BSC is a performance management system that is used to manage the performances of a firm's strategic plan from all four perspectives. The BSC includes the four perspectives, strategic objectives, strategic measures and targets, and strategic initiatives.

STRATEGY MANAGEMENT

EXECUTE

STRATEGIC RISK MANAGEMENT

Strategic risk management is the identification, evaluation, and prioritization of risks within a strategic plan. Leaders must identify and align risk to strategy to drive a sustainable strategic execution. A strategy without strategic risk is a plan without courage; a strategy with identified strategic risk but no mitigating strategies is a strategy that is bound to fail. After the development of a strategic plan, leaders must diligently work to identify strategic risk within a strategic plan and identify ways to mitigate the risk. The question is, however, how much risk is a firm willing to take to achieve its strategic objective?

Bringing strategy and risk close together is fundamentally important. There are three types of organizational risks: known-known, known-unknown, and unknown-unknown. Known-known risks are operational risks, such as employees stealing time. This is a known behavior that is consistent in organizations but mitigated through policies. This behavior does not pose a major threat to an organization.

Unknown-unknown is a risk that leaders cannot predict, such as a natural catastrophe. Although leaders in organizations cannot predict this risk, they can develop catastrophe plans to mitigate the risk in case a natural catastrophe occurs. Strategic risk is considered known-unknown. An example of strategic risk is partnering with a sole-source supplier for a rare item needed to manufacture a product. The strategic risk is that the failure of the sole-source supplier to deliver rare items in a timely fashion or to increase the cost of the rare item can affect a firm's cost and profit margin.

You must create strategies to mitigate known-unknown risks. Failure to rigorously evaluate and challenge risk in a strategic plan is the biggest intellectual failure for leaders. Once you identify known-unknown risks in a strategic plan, you must create contingency plans to mitigate the risk.

Here are a few questions to consider:

1. Identify 3-5 potential strategic risks you see within the strategic plan and explain why using examples of mitigation strategies.

2. Rank the top 3 (in rank order, 1 being the top priority) risks for your area. Explain why you chose these risks.

3. For each risk, do you feel current safeguards (resources, policies/procedures, etc.) are adequate to control the risk? Why or why not?

4. What are barriers or challenges do you foresee in mitigating the identified risks within the strategic plan?

STRATEGIC ALIGNMENT

Strategic alignment is the process of coordinating individual business units to create value for a firm. The coordination of individual business units collectively leverages the products, services, technologies, and competencies of a firm to advance its goals and objectives. Strategic alignment of individual business unit resources with the strategic plan is essential in the strategy management process.

The first step in aligning a firm is to coordinate the resources of all the individual business units. This step creates unity within a firm and helps to lockstep all actions of a firm. The second step is to align the budgeted strategic initiative across a firm using an initiative portfolio. An initiative portfolio is a document that is designed to align the budgeted strategic initiative with executives, individual business unit managers, and initiative owners. When completing an initiative portfolio, assign multiple cross-functional initiatives to foster collaboration across a firm. This document should be completed by senior leaders in a firm. The third step is to align the employees with the individual business unit strategy (See personal scorecards). The third step is to align the review meetings with the strategic plan. The failure to complete these activities can create a misaligned organization. According to Kaplan and Norton, synergy is created through strategic alignment.

You must work together with senior executives to determine which business units must be aligned with the strategic plan, what objectives should cascade down to each business unit, and what internal resources should be shared, combined, leveraged, etc.

STRATEGY MANAGEMENT

Objectives	Duplication	Extension	Business Unit(s)
Financial			
F1. Grow margin	x	x	All Customer Facing Business Units; Operational units must identify cost savings - extension
Stakeholder			
S1. Improve the health and wellness of all Arkansans	x	x	Clinical Programs; Human Resources - extension
Internal Process			
C1. Reduce health disparities across Arkansas	x		Clinical Programs; Regional Programs; Community Clinics
Talent & Technology			
T1. Recruit, develop, and retain a skilled, motivated, and engaged workforce	x		All Busines Units

CASCADING

Cascading objectives from the corporate-parent strategic plan down to a business unit plan is only applicable when a firm has primary and secondary value chains within a firm or when a firm has multiple business sites. According to Jeffery Risinger, leaders must cascade with the intent to create relationships between a firm's corporate plan and its business unit plans. The cascading process includes three options: duplication, extension, and creation. Duplication is the process of identifying strategic objectives in a corporate plan in which individual business units can directly support.

The associated measure(s), target(s), and initiative(s) must be cascaded along with the strategic objectives. Extension is the process of identifying objectives in a corporate plan in which the individual business units can contribute but do not directly support. Creation is the process of creating new objectives that align with a corporate plan and uniquely contribute to the individual business units. When creating new objectives, you must create new measure(s), target(s), and initiative(s) to support the new objectives.

To accelerate this process, you should work with a selected group of senior executives to help you identify the strategic objectives for cascading down to each business unit.

STRATEGY MANAGEMENT

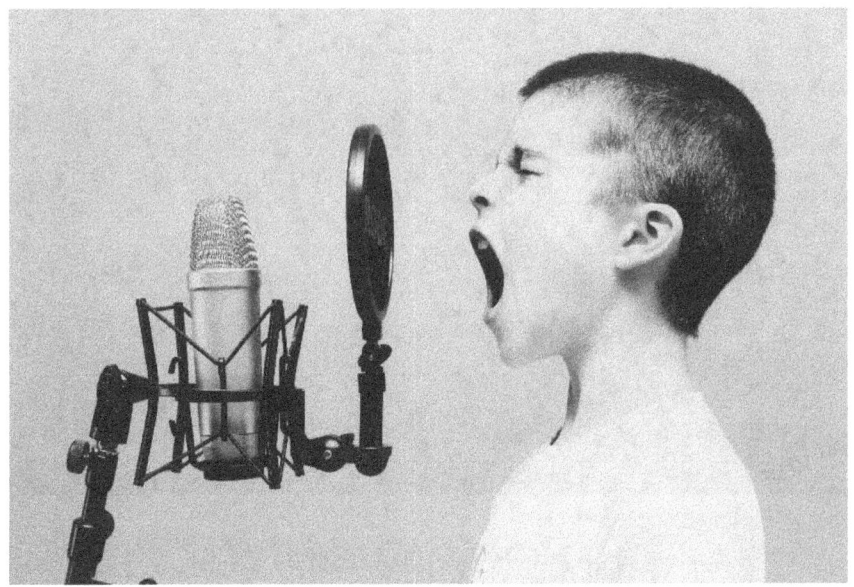

COMMUNICATION PLAN

Creating a communication plan is crucial for engaging stakeholders in the strategic management process. Effective communication includes key executive sponsors, key messages to specific groups, communication channels, and a timeline for received communications.

The messages must consistently inform of the progress of the plan, mitigate potential employee resistance, engage, and inspire internal and external stakeholders. According to research, employees prefer to receive their message from their direct supervisor. All messages must be written for specific groups such as board members, staff, employees, the local community, etc. to get buy-in.

The frequency and medium in which the message is communicated are key factors. According to research, key messages must be communicated at least 5 to 7 times to cement the message. There is no one size fits all method, but research suggests that face-to-face talks (i.e., town hall, group small meetings, videos, etc.) remain the most powerful method for communicating. Lastly, the message must be aligned with the review dates of the strategic plan to ensure that stakeholders are well informed of the progress of the strategy.

CHANGE MANAGEMENT

Mobilizing change is essential in the strategy management process. Change is inevitable in all organizations and it is impossible without the help of employees. Identifying executive sponsors, creating sponsor roadmaps, training, and developing functional managers, and assessing behaviors of employees in the cycle of change are imperative. Functional managers are individual business unit managers who are heavily transactional and responsible for the day-to-day operations of a firm.

According to research, the functional manager is the preferred senders of messages to frontline staff and employees. They manage the process and supervise the work of the frontline staff and/or employees. They are the gateway to employee change. Helping functional managers understand the barriers to change such as awareness, desire, knowledge, ability, and reinforcement is essential for strategy execution. Since the functional manager's goal is to help executives achieve their strategic outcomes, they must be trained on resistance management so that they know what resistance looks like and how to mitigate it. Resistance management refers to the influencing of employee attitudes, behaviors, and actions towards the introduction of change within an organization. The goal of resistance management is to facilitate the adoption of new changes in a firm with minimal friction.

Perspective	Objective	Measure	Target	Employee Performance
Financial	Be awarded Balanced Scorecard Hall of Fame	Effectively manage the process of the Balanced Scorecard	By 2021, attain Hall of Fame award	Successfully manage the parent strategy plan
Internal Process	Provide thought leadership for leaders	Number and type of strategic engagements	By May 2020, complete 200 strategy plans	Educate leaders on the BSC methodology
Talent & Technology	Learn research protocols for publishing			Enroll into the Teaching Scholars program

PERSONAL SCORECARD

The functional manager guides the day-to-day operations of a firm and supervises staff and/or employee work performances. functional managers are responsible for managing and assigning strategic priorities to their employees. They are also responsible for increasing the level of engagement of their employees. According to an independent survey, employees are more engaged in a firm when they know how their day-to-day work contributes to the growth of a firm. The personal scorecard (PS) provides the answer to help engage employees.

PS are performance sheets that align employees to the firm's strategic plan. The goal of the PS is to help set the strategic direction for staff and/or employees to help advance the firm's goals. PS aligns staff and/or employees with the individual business unit strategy.

The PS consists of personal objectives, measures, and targets. The employees bear the responsibility of managing their PS. The PS is created by the functional manager and the staff and/or employee who is assigned a PS.

MANAGE

GOVERNANCE CALENDAR

The dates of targets, milestones, and etcetera within a strategic plan must be integrated into a governance calendar to align a strategic plan to a strategic review meeting. A governance calendar is designed to ensure that reporting alignment by coordinating the dates of a firm's strategic plan with the dates for the individual business unit plans.

The governance calendar gives leaders a line of sight and control of a firm's strategic plan. The governance calendar also holds executives accountable for their role in the strategic plan. Executives must be accountable and responsible for sections of the plan in which they oversee, and they must report on their progress at each strategy review meeting.

You must establish reporting dates in your firm's strategic plan. You must also work with individual business unit leaders to coordinate the dates of each business unit plan with the dates of a firm's strategic plan.

STRATEGY REVIEW

Strategy review meetings should be scheduled quarterly and/or semi-annually. In these meetings, business unit leaders come together to discuss the progress of objectives, targets, and initiatives. These meetings are led by the Chief Executive of the firm. These meetings are designed for intense strategic discussions for iterative learning and are a time when business unit leaders share information with other leaders and receive feedback.

You must attend the strategy review meeting to report on the progress of the strategic plan, learn from the outcomes, and make decisions on the direction of a firm. Reporting the progress of a strategic plan is an in-depth analysis of the performances of strategic objectives and initiatives. You must be able to perform objective-initiative level performance analysis and recommendations. See the questions for performing in-depth analysis for a strategic review.

You must also work with the Communication Department to create a report for communicating the performance and progress of the strategic plan. This report must be distributed to executives across the firm to ensure that all executives are communicating the same message. All executives must march to the same beat.

STRATEGY REFRESH

The strategy refresh meeting must be scheduled annually. In these meetings, the existing strategy is tested. New market data and internal data are introduced to leaders who are challenged to make sense of the data in the strategic context of the organization. The market is agile and moves constantly. Leaders who fail to remain adaptive to market trends are leaders who fail to exist. In this meeting, the strategists facilitate activities such as scenario planning and wargaming to pressure test the existing strategic plans and make adaptations accordingly. The changes to the plan are communicated to all stakeholders and appear as redline edits in the plan.

You must conduct onsite interviews with executives to solicit more insight and perspective on future strategies regarding any change in the external environment. You must work with other leaders to pressure test the current strategic plan using war game methodologies or any method designed to test the viability of the strategy. You must use the results of the war game to conduct a scenario planning activity or market analysis activity to learn about the new changes in the environment. If there are any changes in the plan, you must create redline edits in the plan and work with the Communication Department to publish and communicate the changes to all stakeholders in the firm.

STRATEGY MANAGEMENT

Strategy Review/Refresh Meeting Information Sheet

Types of Meetings / Format	Operations Review	Strategy Review	Strategy Refresh
Information requirements	Dashboard for key performance indicators (KPIs); weekly monthly financial summaries	Strategy map and strategy scorecard reports	Strategy map, balanced scorecard, profitability reports, analytic studies of strategic hypotheses, and external competitive analysis
Frequency	Daily, twice weekly, or monthly	Monthly or quarterly	Semi-annual or annual
Attendees	Departmental and functional personnel; senior management for financial review	Senior mgmt. team, strategic theme owners, strategy mgmt. officer, cross functional, multiple business units	Senior mgmt. team, strategic theme owners, functional and planning specialist, business unit heads
Focus	Identify and solve operational problems	Identify and analyze implementation issues and make decisions to move the strategy forward	Test and adapt strategy based on casual analytics; use scenario planning to evaluate tail risk events; war games to test against competitor's strategies
Goal	Respond to short-term problems and promote continuous improvements	Fine-tune strategy; make midcourse adaptations	Improve or transform strategy

ABOUT THE AUTHOR

Dr. Mario D. Wallace, founder of the All-Things Strategic brand, has more than 20 years of small business consulting experience and 11 years of healthcare consulting experience. He has considerable expertise in the areas of process improvement, change management, leadership development, medical education, program instructional development, strategic management, and product development. Recently, he published the books *Strategy Is Spelled ADEM,* the *Unstoppable Leader*, and the Executive Performance Journal.

Dr. Wallace earned his bachelor's degrees in International Language and Rhetoric and Writing and his master's degree in Education from the University of Arkansas at Little Rock. He earned his doctoral degree from Walden University in Business Administration Leadership. He has certifications in the Balanced Scorecard from Palladium Group, Lean Six Sigma Black Belt from Villanova University, Change Management from PROSCI, Emotional Intelligence from the Hay Group, Communication from the Wiley Everything DISC Workplace, and Facilitation from Development Dimension International (DDI). Dr. Wallace also earned his COVID-19 Contract Tracing Certificate from Johns Hopkins University.

BOOKING INFORMATION

All Things Strategic makes it easy to book Dr. Mario Wallace for book tours and local book signings, corporate events, private events, social media campaigns, appearances, speaking engagements, workshops, and product endorsements worldwide.

Mario Wallace can also be booked for private virtual appearances and live streams. Start by emailing allthingsstrategic@gmail.com or give us a call at (501) 551-9170 and one of our booking agents will be happy to assist.

Monday-Friday 9:00 AM-7:00 PM.

SERVICES

Strategic Planning

Strategic planning is the process of analyzing market data and internal factors and making decisions to chart a path to expand markets, compete within markets, disrupt markets, and/or create a networking market. It is also about choosing a unique and valuable position rooted in systems of activities that are difficult to match. We help business owners, C-level executives, and board members define their strategy, or direction, and make decisions on allocating resources to pursue their strategy. We facilitate strategic planning retreats that include leaders and their implementation teams.

Advising

Our advising services help professionals and organizations effectively navigate business risks and opportunities—including strategic and operational (e.g., change management, project management, and process improvement) risks—to gain and sustain competitive advantage. We apply our experience in ongoing business strategies and operations to help clients become stronger and more resilient and to make competitors irrelevant.

Assessments

Our consultants administer a wide array of assessments that will aid in personal and team development, and a systematic process for evaluating process inefficiencies and potential strategic or operational risks.

All consultants are certified in Lean Six Sigma, Wiley's Workplace DiSC, Hay Group's Emotional and Social Competency Inventory, Wallace's OPDC Strategic Thinking Assessment, and Wallace's ADEM Readiness Assessment.

Workshops

Our interactive workshops are facilitated by certified experts in their field and subject who collaboratively design their material to help professionals and organizations create a culture of employee engagement and strong leadership.

Strategic Thinking

Strategic thinking is a rational decision-making process that focuses on sensing, analyzing, and reconfiguring ideas, concepts, and strategies to create new ways of doing business that differentiates a firm from its competitor. In this workshop, the facilitator discusses ways to improve one's strategic thinking skills and teaches practical strategic thinking methods to maximize business decisions. Participants complete an OPDC (operation, planning, discovery, and creation) strategic thinking assessment to learn their own strategic thinking capabilities and to create an action plan to strengthen their strategic thinking skills.

Becoming a Strategically Aligned Business

The facilitator uses concepts from Kaplan-Norton's Balanced Scorecard framework to educate participants on the elements of a strategy-focused firm. Participants gain knowledge and practical application of aligning a firm's internal resources, translating strategy across a firm, and creating personal scorecards for their employees. Participants will also learn the role that culture plays in creating a strategy-focused organization.

Generational Differences

The facilitator lays out the differences amongst generations using historical elements that support each generation's beliefs, politics, or values. The facilitator also teaches strategies to leverage positive interactions between generations.

Positive Interpersonal Communication

The facilitator lays out the 7 elements of positive communication using the Dr. Julien Mirivel's Model of Positive Communication. Participants learn how to engage customers, co-workers, partners, and business partners in a positive interaction. Participants complete the DiSC Communication Style Assessment and learn their preferred communication style and how to determine the communication styles of others. Participants learn communication strategies to create a positive working environment.

Emotional Intelligence

The facilitator lays out the four elements of Emotional Intelligence (EI)- self-awareness, self-management, organizational awareness, and relationship management- in an interactive, team-based learning setting. The facilitator teaches strategies for enhancing participant's knowledge and application of EI elements to evaluate personal strengths as well as opportunities for development.

Change Management

The facilitator explains the principles of Change Management using relevant industry-specific case studies. The facilitator teaches core elements that affect organizational change and individual change. Participants learn the five barriers of change and how to leverage them to mitigate resistance. Participants learn how to develop a sponsor roadmap, a communication plan, and a corrective action plan. Participants learn strategies to mitigate employee resistance.

Team Building

The facilitator lays out the elements for fostering a sociable and collaborative workplace to increase productivity. The participants learn strategies to enhance their interpersonal relationships with co-workers to create team spirit, fun, and motivation. The participants also learn strategies to engage the workforce to stimulate innovation, creation, and friendly competition.

www.ingramcontent.com/pod-product-compliance
Lightning Source LLC
Chambersburg PA
CBHW070856220526
45466CB00005B/2011